THE
ASIAN QUESTION COLLECTION

MORE THAN 200 QUESTIONS ABOUT HISTORY, GEOGRAPHY, CUSTOMS, HOLIDAYS & CELEBRATIONS, SPORTS & GAMES, FOOD, AND MORE

Written by Linda Schwartz • Illustrated by Nobue Maeno

The Learning Works

Text Design and Editorial Production: Sherri M. Butterfield
Typesetting: Clark Editorial & Design

Copyright © 1994—Linda Schwartz
THE LEARNING WORKS, INC.
P.O. Box 6187
Santa Barbara, CA 93160
Printed in the United States of America.

Library of Congress Number: 94-077366
ISBN: 0-88160-215-9

Introduction

This book is a collection of more than 200 questions on Asia with specific questions about the Asian countries of Bangladesh, Burma, China, India, Indonesia, Japan, Kampuchea, Mongolia, North Korea, Pakistan, the Philippines, South Korea, Taiwan, and Thailand.

The questions cover a variety of topics including food, clothing, customs, history and heroes, holidays and celebrations, sports and games, religions and rituals, arts and crafts, architecture, geography, places of interest, and more. These questions are intended for use in the classroom, at home, or anywhere that children have empty minutes to fill, and are ideal for keeping kids occupied on rainy days, before recess, or while traveling.

The Asian Question Collection
© 1994—The Learning Works, Inc.

Introduction
(continued)

The questions have been placed two to a page. While an effort has been made to vary both the countries and the topics across a two-page spread, the arrangement of these question is random. Thus, they can be asked and answered in any order.

No collection of questions would be complete without a collection of answers. For this book, the answers appear on pages 109–119. These answers have been listed by page number and keyed by letter to a particular position on the page. Thus, answer **a** is for the question on the left side of the page, and answer **b** is for the question on the right side of the page. See diagram.

a	b

A Special Message to Teachers

The ways to use this book in your classroom are almost endless. To begin with, of course, you can open it to any page and ask a few questions to fill those last few restless minutes before lunch or recess.

You can turn the questions into a self-checking game. Select pages on which the questions are appropriate for the grade level you teach. Duplicate some of these pages, and cut the questions apart. Glue each question to one side of a plain index card. Glue or write the corresponding answer on the other side of the card. Laminate the cards and make them available as part of a classroom display or learning center.

You can turn the process of answering the questions into a research activity. Select pages on which the questions are somewhat challenging for the grade level you teach. Duplicate these pages and make cards but do not write the answers on the cards. Instead, write the corresponding page number and the answer letter (that is, a or b).

The Asian Question Collection
© 1994—The Learning Works, Inc.

A Special Message to Teachers
(continued)

Distribute the cards, and challenge individual students or teams to find and record the answers within some specified period of time. Then, check their results against the answer key. You may want to keep score on a chart or graph by week or month.

Use the question cards to play Asian Answers Tic-Tac-Toe. With ribbon or yarn, make a large tic-tac-toe grid on your multicultural bulletin board. Place one question card in each of the nine squares on the grid. Challenge your students—working alone or in teams—to find the answers to any three questions that will give them three in a row horizontally, vertically, or diagonally.

You can use questions on a particular topic as part of a classroom display on that topic. Look through the book and select a group of questions that are related by topic.

A Special Message to Teachers

(continued)

For example, you might select questions about a specific country or about the history, heroes, or holidays of the entire region. Duplicate the pages on which these questions appear. Cut out the questions you have selected, and post them on a classroom bulletin board or wall. Make blank cards available, and suggest that students write and illustrate additional questions about the same topic for the display.

In addition, you can use these questions for question bees, for staged classroom quiz shows that follow a radio or television format, and as challenging bonus activities for students who have completed their assignments and are looking for something more to do. In short, you may find that this Asian question collection provides a lot of answers for a busy teacher with a bustling classroom.

The Asian Question Collection
© 1994—The Learning Works, Inc.

A Special Message to Parents

The ways to use this book are almost endless. It's perfect for increasing multicultural awareness, filling indoor time on rainy days, amusing a child who is ill, or making the miles go faster when you travel. For example, your child might use the questions it contains to stage a quiz show in radio or television format. For a change, let your child be the quiz master while you play contestant and try to supply the answers.

Use selected questions as a party game. Choose teams, ask questions, keep score, and reward the winners with prizes of some kind. Use this book to sharpen research skills. If your child does not know an answer, instead of revealing it, help him or her look it up in a dictionary, encyclopedia, or other similar reference book. You can also use this book as the inspiration for an art activity. Supply plain index cards and a black felt-tipped marking pen, and encourage your child to add to this Asian question collection.

Instead of forks,
what do many
Asian people eat with?

Which country is known as
the Land of the Rising Sun?

The Asian Question Collection
© 1994—The Learning Works, Inc.

What is the capital
of China?

Which famous building in India
was constructed by Shah Jahan
as a tomb for his wife and himself?

What is the Japanese art
of paper folding called?

In the Hindu religion,
what name is given
to the process by which
the soul is reborn
in another form
when the body dies?

The Asian Question Collection
© 1994—The Learning Works, Inc.

Was Confucius a famous Chinese doctor, farmer, or teacher?

Tokyo is the capital of which country?

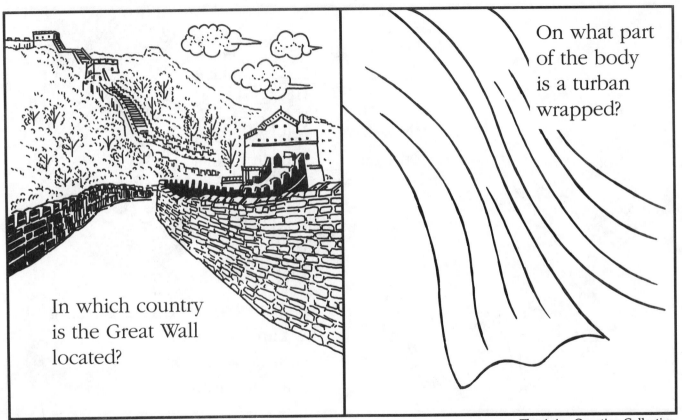

In which country is the Great Wall located?

On what part of the body is a turban wrapped?

13

The Asian Question Collection
© 1994—The Learning Works, Inc.

What is
the official language
of Vietnam?

Đây là con gì?

Đây là con trâu.

Are Ling-Ling and Hsing-Hsing
the names of Chinese
cities, dancers, or
giant pandas?

What origami bird
has become a symbol of peace
for Japanese children?

What Chinese holiday occurs
on the first day
of the first lunar month?

The Asian Question Collection
© 1994—The Learning Works, Inc.

Does the Japanese word **sake** name a dessert, a drink, or a robe?

What two colors are found on the flag of Indonesia?

What Korean form of karate emphasizes spectacular kicks?

What does the giant panda eat?

The Asian Question Collection
© 1994—The Learning Works, Inc.

What is a Moslem
house of worship
called?

Which ocean separates
Japan from the United States?

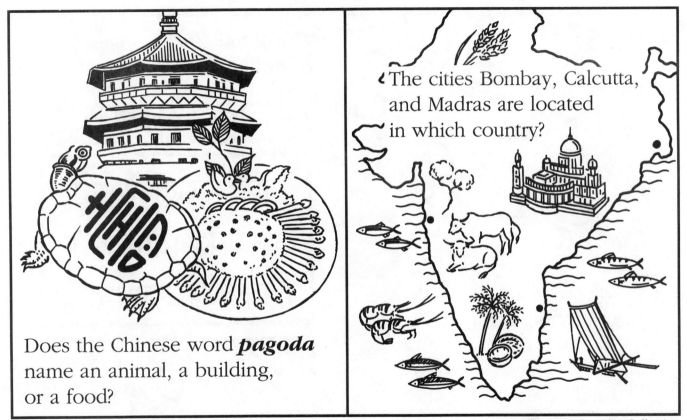

Does the Chinese word **pagoda** name an animal, a building, or a food?

The cities Bombay, Calcutta, and Madras are located in which country?

The Asian Question Collection
© 1994—The Learning Works, Inc.

古池や
蛙とびこむ
水の音

Which form of Japanese poetry is written in three lines, contains seventeen syllables, and usually describes nature?

What is the official language of northern India?

धीसेकट उसदयठवे

आपनी नकदी और जेवर
का आप खयाल रग्वे
जेवकतरो से साबधान रहे

اینی نقدی أور زیور کا

What is the highest mountain in Japan?

What name is given to the Indian practice of training both the body and the mind?

The Asian Question Collection
© 1994—The Learning Works, Inc.

On which holiday
do Chinese children receive
red envelopes filled with money?

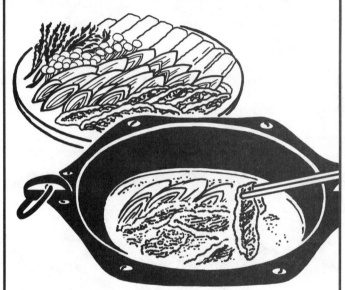

Is a popular Japanese dish
made by boiling beef strips
with bean curds called
samurai, sukiyaki, or sushi?

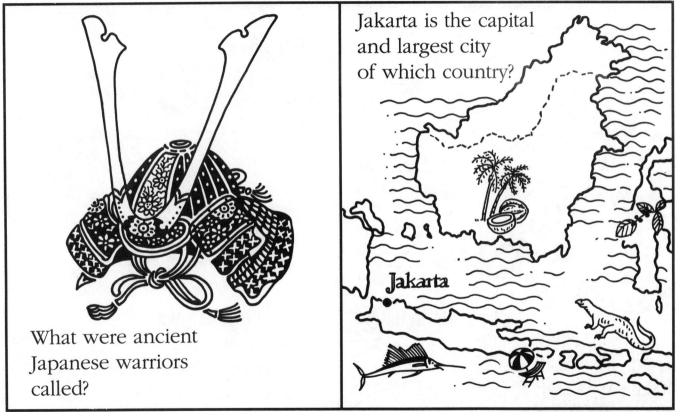

What were ancient
Japanese warriors
called?

Jakarta is the capital
and largest city
of which country?

Jakarta

The Asian Question Collection
© 1994—The Learning Works, Inc.

Shanghai and Tianjin (or Tientsin) are cities in which country?

Tianjin

Shanghai

What name is given to the seasonal winds that bring heavy summer rains to southern Asia?

What are the colorful,
wrapped skirts worn by
Indonesian women called?

What name is given
to the ancient Chinese art
of writing with a brush
in ink on special paper?

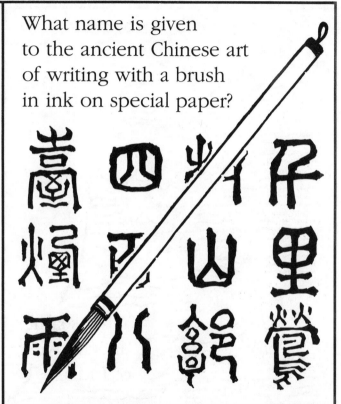

The Asian Question Collection
© 1994—The Learning Works, Inc.

What sea lies directly west of India?

Which of these words names a spicy Indian dish made with meat, fish, eggs, or vegetables and served over rice: chutney, curry, or sari?

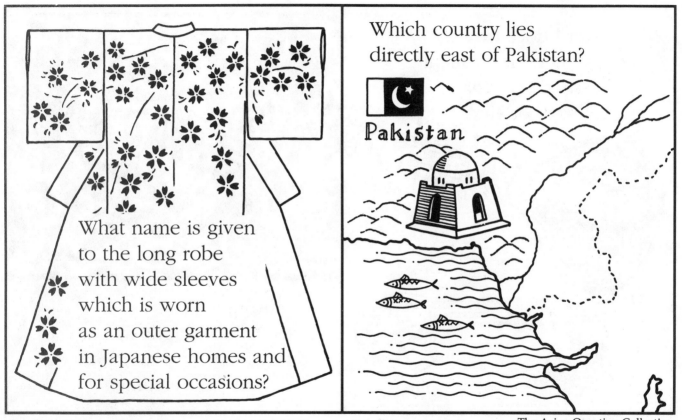

What name is given
to the long robe
with wide sleeves
which is worn
as an outer garment
in Japanese homes and
for special occasions?

Which country lies
directly east of Pakistan?

Pakistan

The Asian Question Collection
© 1994—The Learning Works, Inc.

Which word does **not** name a stringed instrument found in southern Asia: lute, sari, sitar, or vina?

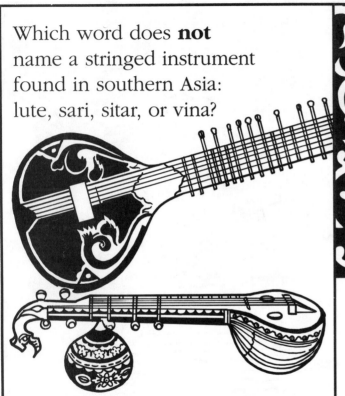

Muslim males try to make a pilgrimage to which city at least once during their lifetime?

The milk of what nut
is an important ingredient
in many Indonesian dishes?

Tibet

Himalayas

Nepal

The highest mountain
in the world
is in the Himalayas,
between Tibet and Nepal.
What is the name
of this famous peak?

The Asian Question Collection
© 1994—The Learning Works, Inc.

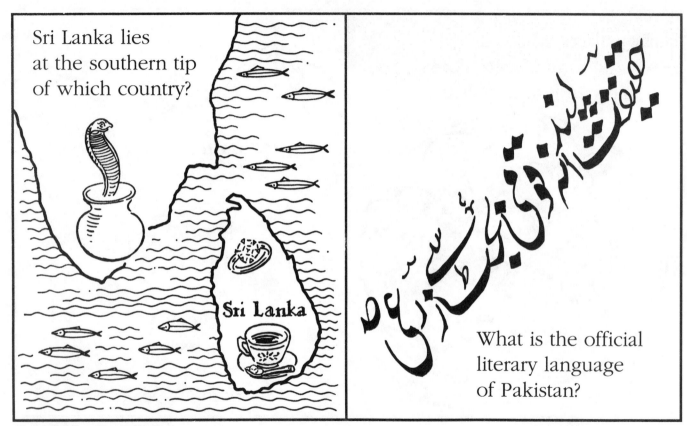

Sri Lanka lies
at the southern tip
of which country?

Sri Lanka

What is the official
literary language
of Pakistan?

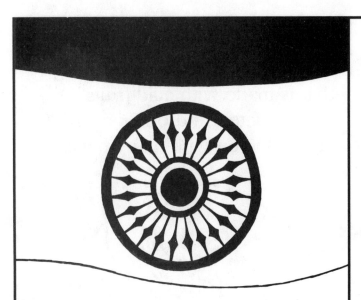

What symbol
is found in the center
of India's flag?

Which hand do people
in Muslim nations
always use for eating?

31

The Asian Question Collection
© 1994—The Learning Works, Inc.

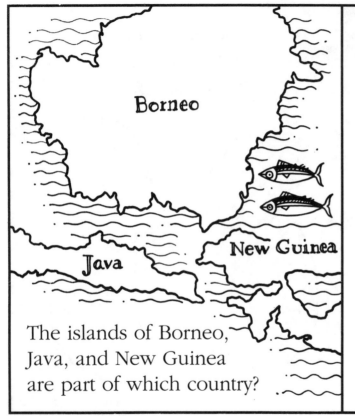

The islands of Borneo, Java, and New Guinea are part of which country?

What name is given to the spicy Indian relish that is made with acid fruits, raisins, dates, and onions and is served with many meals?

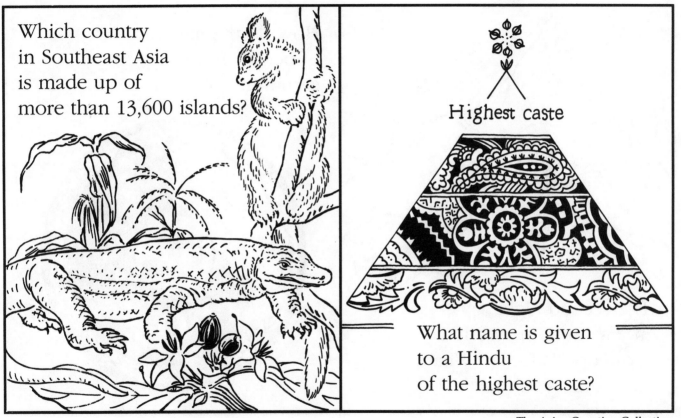

Which country
in Southeast Asia
is made up of
more than 13,600 islands?

Highest caste

What name is given
to a Hindu
of the highest caste?

The Asian Question Collection
© 1994—The Learning Works, Inc.

The second highest mountain in the world is located in Pakistan. What is the name of this peak?

How do the majority of people in India earn a living?

70%

In Japan, would you eat, plant, or wear *geta*?

Many Chinese people believe that the universe is made up of what two opposing forces?

35

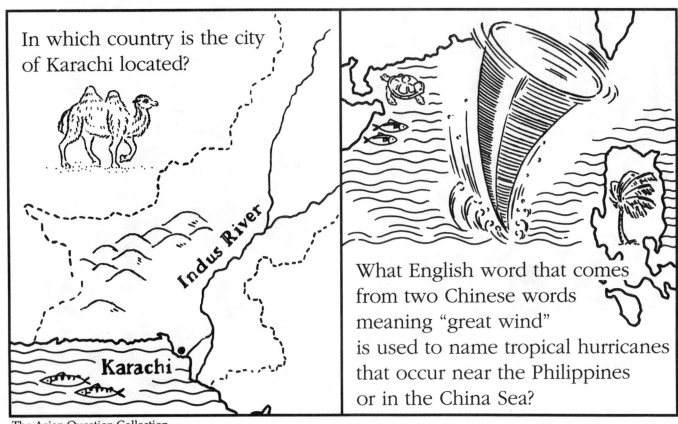

In which country is the city of Karachi located?

Indus River

Karachi

What English word that comes from two Chinese words meaning "great wind" is used to name tropical hurricanes that occur near the Philippines or in the China Sea?

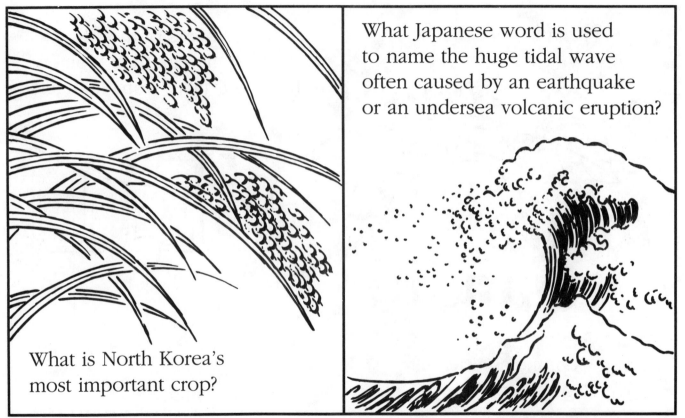

What Japanese word is used to name the huge tidal wave often caused by an earthquake or an undersea volcanic eruption?

What is North Korea's most important crop?

The Asian Question Collection
© 1994—The Learning Works, Inc.

Indira Gandhi

Indira Gandhi
served as prime minister
of which Asian country?

What is the name of the veil
worn by some Pakistani women
to hide their faces from strangers?

VEIL

这 是 什 么 年 代 的 ？

What is the official
language of China?

Haiphong, Hanoi, and
Ho Chi Minh are
cities in which country?

39

What is the name
of the holy book of Islam?

What name is given
to a Japanese soup
made of broth, soybean paste,
and vegetables or seaweed?

What Chinese method
of treating pain and illness
relies on fine needles
to stimulate pressure points
on the body?

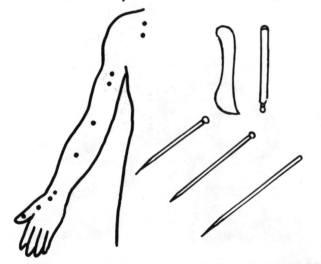

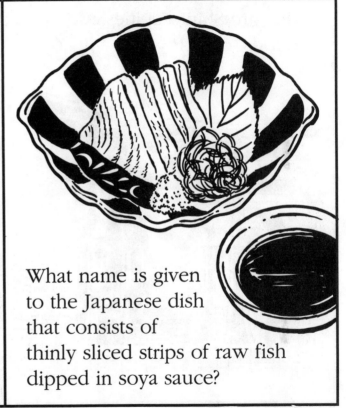

What name is given
to the Japanese dish
that consists of
thinly sliced strips of raw fish
dipped in soya sauce?

The Asian Question Collection
© 1994—The Learning Works, Inc.

What are Shinto deities, or gods, called?

What is the name of the ninth month of the Muslim year?

What is the name
of the sweet pastries
eaten during the Chinese
Harvest Moon Festival?

Which group of men
on the Indian subcontinent
never cut their hair
or shave their beards?

43

The Asian Question Collection
© 1994—The Learning Works, Inc.

What is the name of the stew made with chicken and pork that is the national dish of the Philippines?

What system of government is found in India, Japan, and the Philippines?

INDIA

JAPAN

PHILIPPINES

What was the given name
of the Chinese religious leader
known as the Buddha,
or Enlightened One?

Which Asian game
resembles volleyball?

The Asian Question Collection
© 1994—The Learning Works, Inc.

What name is given
to the form of government
in which a ruler—such as a king,
queen, or emperor—
holds power for life?

Whose teachings
were collected
into the Five Books
of Chinese classics?

Indonesian students in Bali, Java, and Sumatra enjoy a sport that combines self-defense and dancing. What is this sport called?

Sumatra

Java

Bali

In India, is the Deccan a huge plateau, a river, or a famous shrine?

The Asian Question Collection
© 1994—The Learning Works, Inc.

What is the name
of the traditional
long, full skirt that
Korean women wear?

What are flat-bottomed
Chinese houseboats
called?

What Chinese game is played
with 144 decorated tiles
that are drawn and discarded
until one player secures
a winning hand?

In India, who was known
as the Mahatma,
or Great Soul?

49

The Asian Question Collection
© 1994—The Learning Works, Inc.

In India, is a **guru** a ceremonial dance, a wise teacher, or an exotic vegetable?

What is the capital city of South Korea?

Which two creatures
are most often featured
in Chinese New Year parades?

What is the name
of the Japanese bean-curd cake
made from ground soybeans?

The Asian Question Collection
© 1994—The Learning Works, Inc.

What is another name
for tall, slender, balconied
towers like those found
at each corner of the Taj Mahal?

What is the major religion
of India?

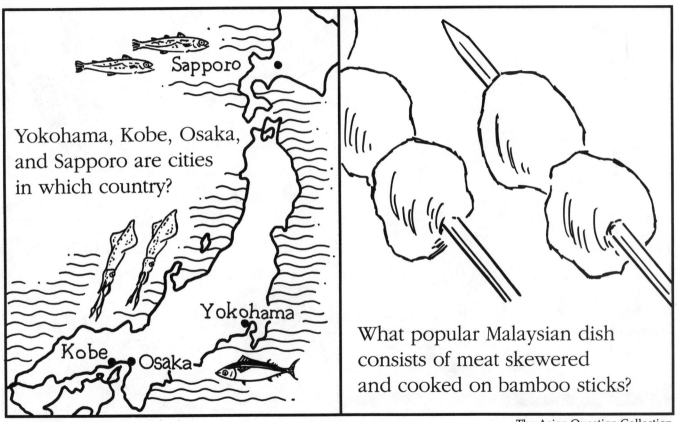

Yokohama, Kobe, Osaka, and Sapporo are cities in which country?

Sapporo

Yokohama

Kobe

Osaka

What popular Malaysian dish consists of meat skewered and cooked on bamboo sticks?

53

The Asian Question Collection
© 1994—The Learning Works, Inc.

What name is given to the straw matting used as a floor covering in many Japanese homes?

According to the Asian lunar calendar, each year is represented by a different animal. How many years, and animals, make up a single cycle?

Benazir Bhutto served
as prime minister
of which Asian nation?

In which Malaysian folk art
is a wax-and-dye process used
to create designs on fabric?

55

What is the name
of the broad sash worn
on a Japanese robe?

What is China's
largest city and
major port?

What is a series
of Chinese rulers
from the same family
called?

Corazon Aquino
was the president
of which Asian nation?

The Asian Question Collection
© 1994—The Learning Works, Inc.

Which popular Japanese sport began as a religious ritual to amuse the Shinto gods?

大相撲

What large mountain range is found in northern India?

Japan is made up of how many main islands?

When do the Chinese celebrate Liberation Day?

59

The Hindu Festival of Lights
is called Diwali.
For how many days
does this festival last?

What is the name
of the famous Chinese canal
that stretches from Beijing
to Hangzhou?

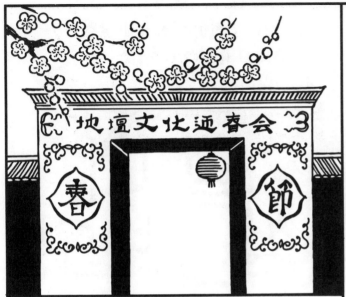

What popular Chinese holiday comes two weeks after the Spring Festival?

Nippon
is another name
for which country?

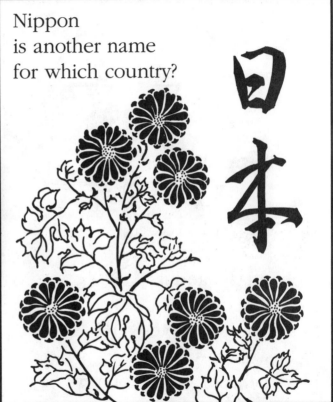

The Asian Question Collection
© 1994—The Learning Works, Inc.

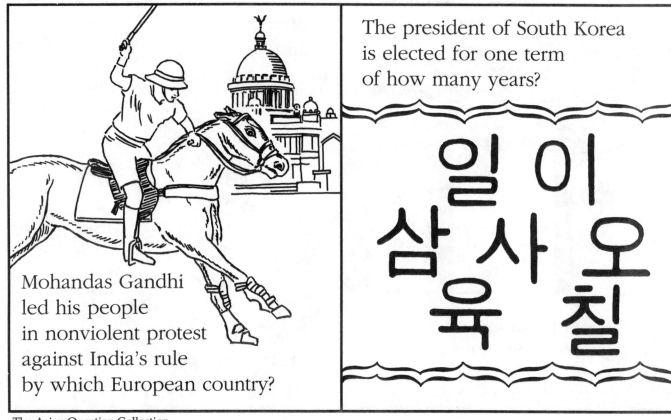

The president of South Korea is elected for one term of how many years?

일 이
삼 사 오
육 칠

Mohandas Gandhi
led his people
in nonviolent protest
against India's rule
by which European country?

On which Japanese holiday do young girls set up a display of their family's collection of antique and heirloom dolls dressed in traditional costume?

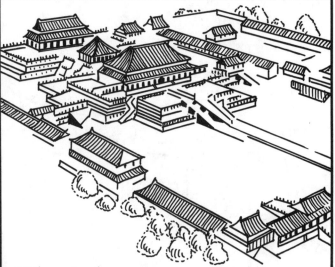

What is the name of the walled group of palaces and museums in Beijing which once served as the emperor's residence?

The Asian Question Collection
© 1994—The Learning Works, Inc.

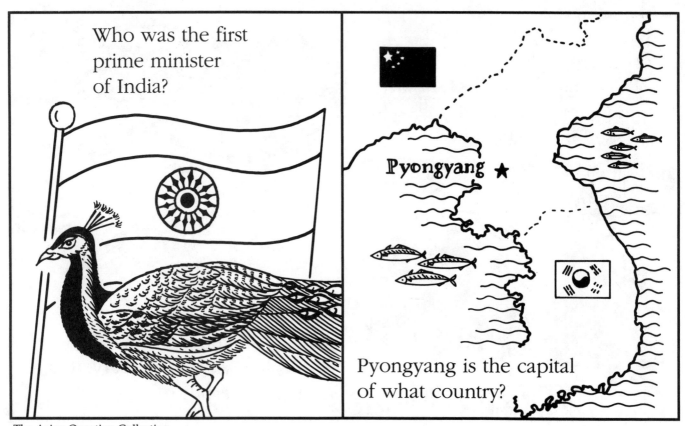

Who was the first
prime minister
of India?

Pyongyang

Pyongyang is the capital
of what country?

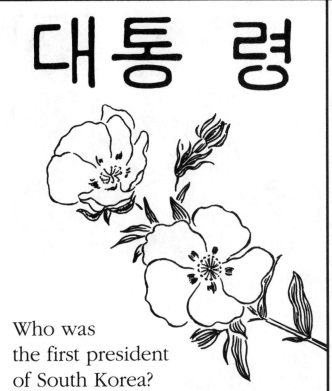

대통령

Who was
the first president
of South Korea?

The Japanese holiday
called Otori Sama
celebrates the spirit
of what two things?

65

How many major dynasties
are found in Chinese history?

What word names a form
of Japanese drama that
is based on old themes and
performed according to tradition:
Kabuki, Karate, or Kobe?

Chinese music
is based on a scale
with how many tones?

The Japanese celebrate
Sports Day for children.
What is this event called?

67

The Asian Question Collection
© 1994—The Learning Works, Inc.

What is the basic unit of money in India?

What name is given to Korean ballads that are chanted by traveling minstrels to the beat of drums?

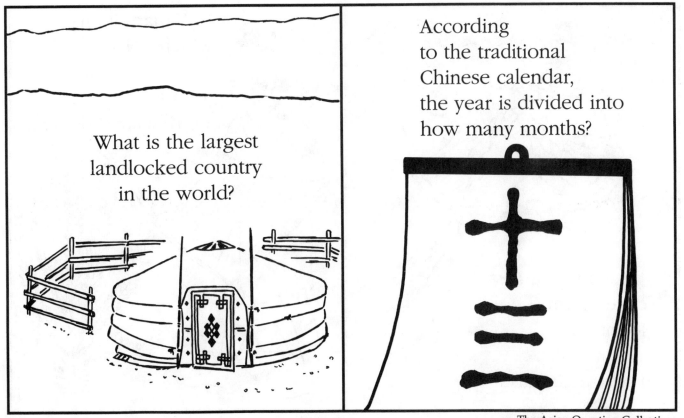

What is the largest
landlocked country
in the world?

According
to the traditional
Chinese calendar,
the year is divided into
how many months?

The Asian Question Collection
© 1994—The Learning Works, Inc.

The world's largest
active volcano,
Mount Aso,
is located
in which country?

In Indian drama,
which hero
rescues his wife
from Ravana,
a ten-headed demon?

What famous Japanese-American architect designed the two-towered World Trade Center in New York City?

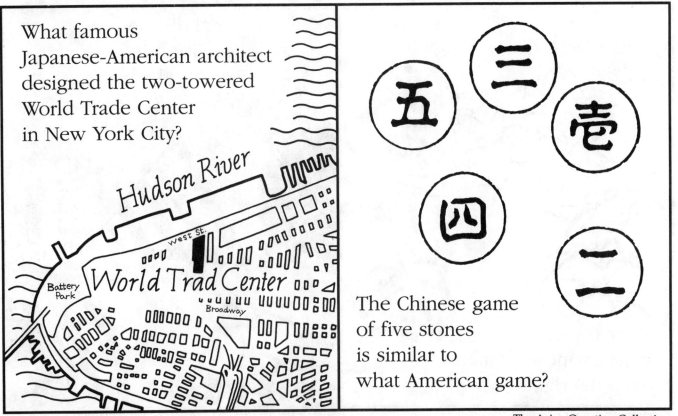

Hudson River

West St.

World Trad Center

Battery Park

Broadway

The Chinese game of five stones is similar to what American game?

The Asian Question Collection
© 1994—The Learning Works, Inc.

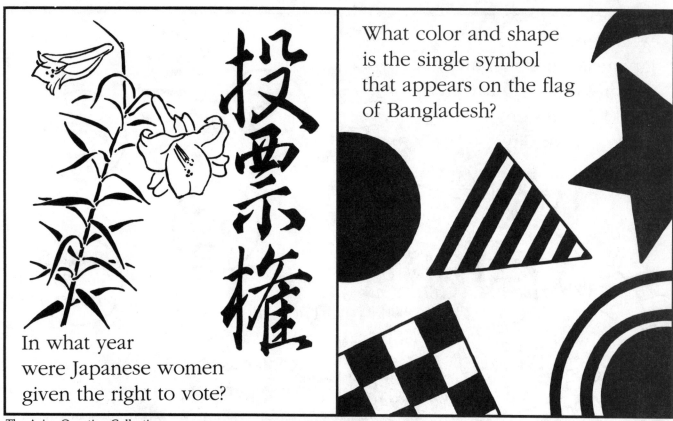

投票権

In what year were Japanese women given the right to vote?

What color and shape is the single symbol that appears on the flag of Bangladesh?

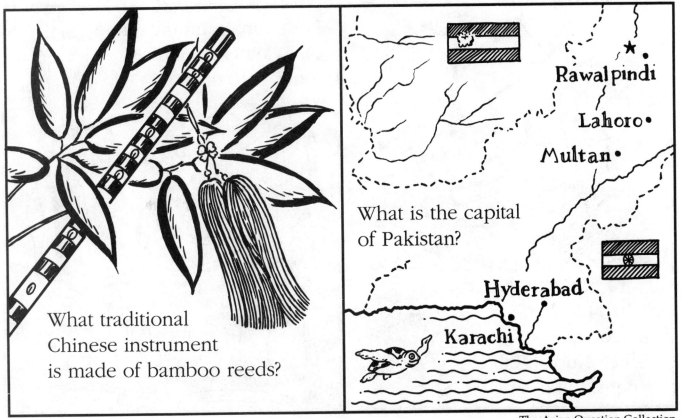

What traditional Chinese instrument is made of bamboo reeds?

What is the capital of Pakistan?

Rawalpindi

Lahore

Multan

Hyderabad

Karachi

The Asian Question Collection
© 1994—The Learning Works, Inc.

In 1275, when the Italian traveler, Marco Polo, visited Kublai Kahn, where was he?

Is Brahmaputra the name of a Chinese building, food, god, or river?

Through which countries does the Indus River flow?

Indus River

What is Japan's second largest island?

The Asian Question Collection
© 1994—The Learning Works, Inc.

Both the Chinese and the Japanese perfected the art of decorating surfaces with raised enamel shapes outlined by soldered metal. What is this art called?

What Japanese educator invented the sport of judo?

The Yangtze and Yellow rivers flow through which country?

What Chinese statesman planned the revolt against the Manchus and is called the "father of the revolution"?

The Asian Question Collection
© 1994—The Learning Works, Inc.

By what other name
is the island of Taiwan
known?

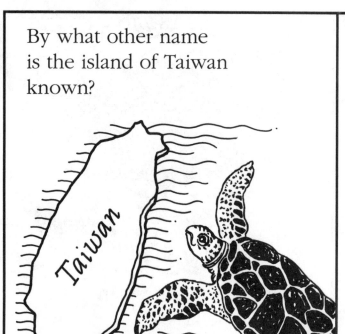

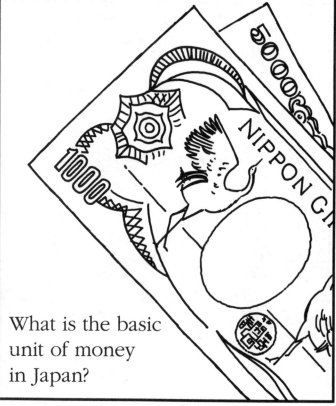

What is the basic
unit of money
in Japan?

What is the name
of Japan's longest river?

共和国万岁　世界人民大团结万岁

Who was the founder of the
Chinese Communist Party?

79

The Asian Question Collection
© 1994—The Learning Works, Inc.

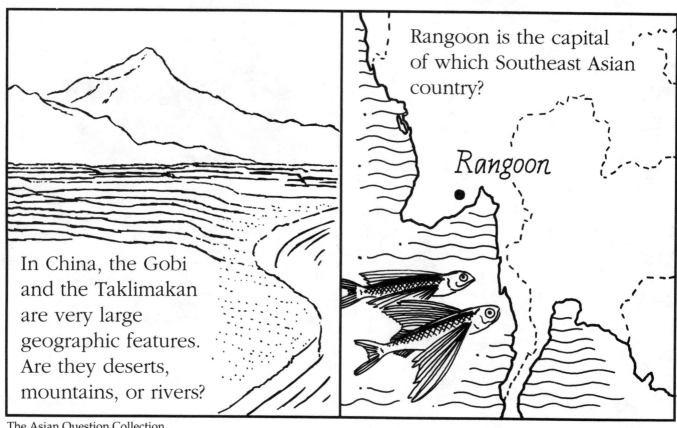

In China, the Gobi and the Taklimakan are very large geographic features. Are they deserts, mountains, or rivers?

Rangoon is the capital of which Southeast Asian country?

Rangoon

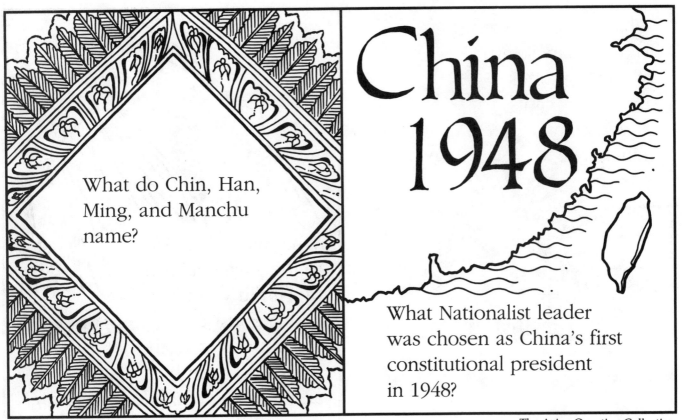

What do Chin, Han, Ming, and Manchu name?

China 1948

What Nationalist leader was chosen as China's first constitutional president in 1948?

The Asian Question Collection
© 1994—The Learning Works, Inc.

What name is given
to the Japanese art
of growing trees
and other plants
as decorative
miniatures?

What name is given
to the garment worn
by Hindu women
which consists of a long piece
of lightweight cloth
draped to form both a skirt
and a head or shoulder covering?

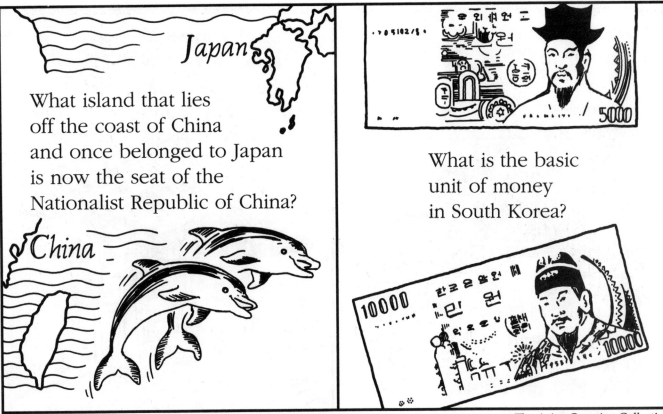

What island that lies off the coast of China and once belonged to Japan is now the seat of the Nationalist Republic of China?

What is the basic unit of money in South Korea?

The Asian Question Collection
© 1994—The Learning Works, Inc.

What name is given to the dome-shaped shrines in which statues and carvings of Buddha are displayed?

Which Japanese religion is based on the worship of the Emperor, ancestors, and spirits of nature?

Which long-haired dog, first bred in China over a thousand years ago, was once considered sacred and is variously known as the Lion Dog, the Sun Dog, and the Sleeve Dog?

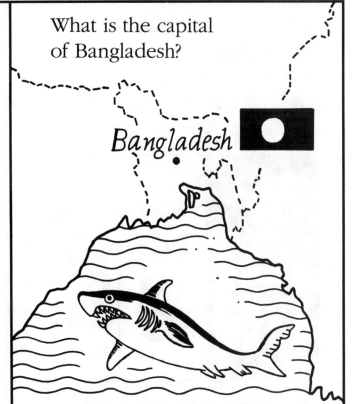

What is the capital of Bangladesh?

Bangladesh

85

Who was the leader
of the Mongol army
that invaded China
in 1279 and established
the Yuan dynasty?

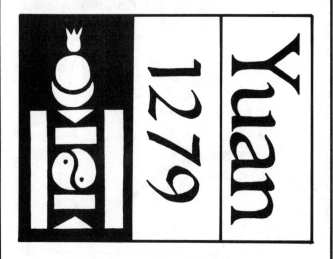

What two things
does the color white
on South Korea's flag
represent?

The Huang Ho,
or Huang Hu,
is a river in China.
By what other name
is this river known?

What name is given
to the sliding doors
found in traditional
Japanese homes?

The Asian Question Collection
© 1994—The Learning Works, Inc.

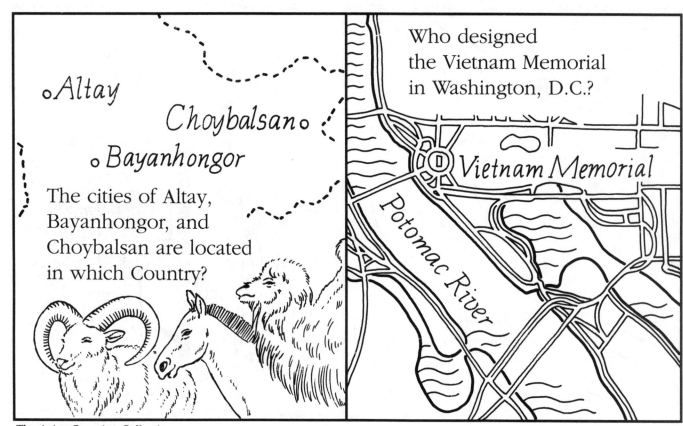

Altay

Choybalsan

Bayanhongor

The cities of Altay, Bayanhongor, and Choybalsan are located in which Country?

Who designed the Vietnam Memorial in Washington, D.C.?

Vietnam Memorial

Potomac River

The Han, Kum, and Naktong
are rivers in which country?

What is the name given
to the flat, thonged sandals,
made of straw, leather, or rubber,
which are worn by the Japanese?

The Asian Question Collection
© 1994—The Learning Works, Inc.

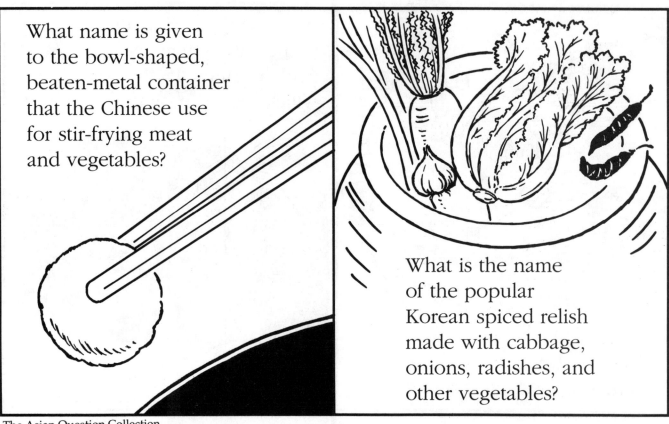

What name is given to the bowl-shaped, beaten-metal container that the Chinese use for stir-frying meat and vegetables?

What is the name of the popular Korean spiced relish made with cabbage, onions, radishes, and other vegetables?

What holiday is celebrated in mid-April to welcome the Burmese New Year?

The Indus, the Ganges, and the Brahmaputra are rivers found in which Asian nation?

Indus

Brahmaputra

Ganges

The Asian Question Collection
© 1994—The Learning Works, Inc.

Which Korean
musical instrument
consists of sixteen bells
hung in two rows
on a wooden stand?

What does the red star
on the flag of North Korea
represent?

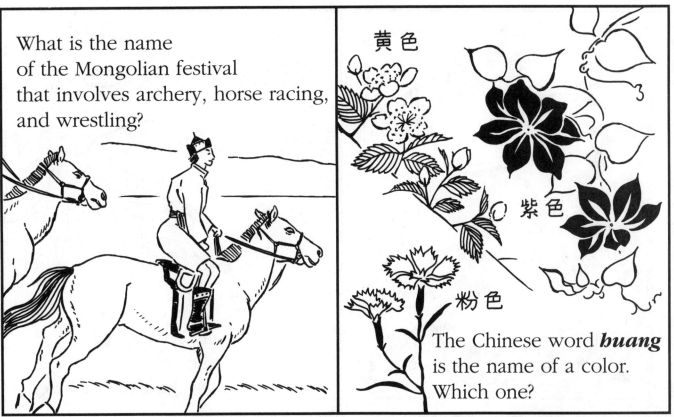

What is the name
of the Mongolian festival
that involves archery, horse racing,
and wrestling?

黄色

紫色

粉色

The Chinese word *huang*
is the name of a color.
Which one?

The Asian Question Collection
© 1994—The Learning Works, Inc.

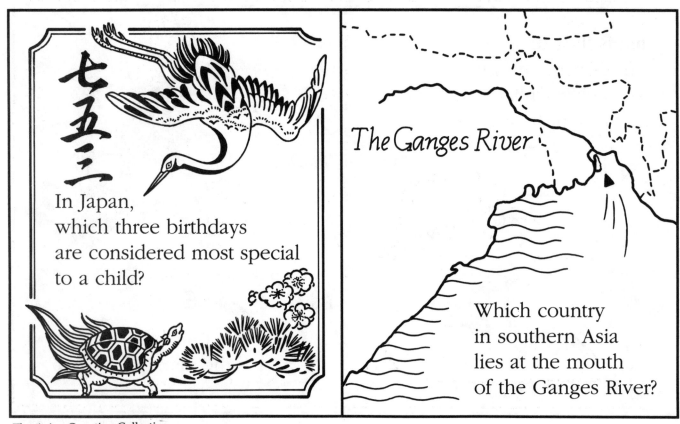

七五三

In Japan,
which three birthdays
are considered most special
to a child?

The Ganges River

Which country
in southern Asia
lies at the mouth
of the Ganges River?

What name is given to the versatile piece of upholstered furniture, designed by the Japanese, which can be unfolded to make a bed or folded to make a chair?

There is a book entitled *Anna and the King of Siam.* By what name is the ancient country of Siam known today?

The Asian Question Collection
© 1994—The Learning Works, Inc.

The highest price
ever paid at auction
for a ceramic piece
was $1,296,000
for a Ming vase.
In which Asian country
was this vase created?

Are **soba** and **udon**
types of flowers,
noodles, or nuts?

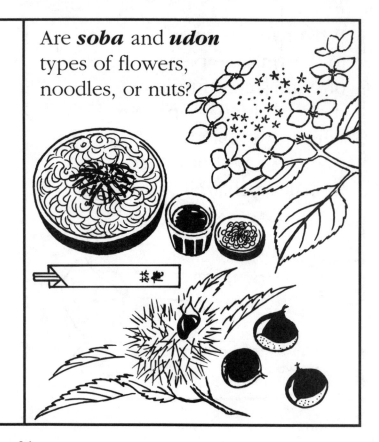

Which Asian country lies directly south of Mongolia?

Mongolia

What name is given to the traditional tall, wide-brimmed hat worn by Korean men?

The Asian Question Collection
© 1994—The Learning Works, Inc.

What is the name of the Asian country that was once known as Cambodia?

Cambodia

Which Chinese holiday takes place in April and honors those who fought and died in the revolutionary war?

四月

The city in Vietnam
which was once
called Saigon
has a new name.
What is it?

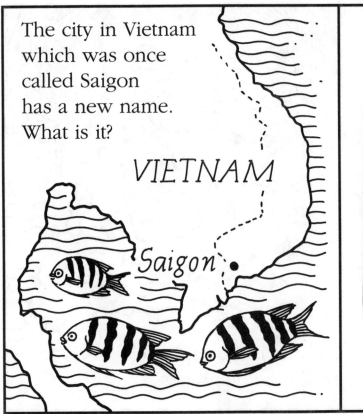

VIETNAM

Saigon

The Bon Festival,
celebrated in July,
honors Japanese
ancestors.
By what other name
is this festival known?

The Asian Question Collection
© 1994—The Learning Works, Inc.

In Korea,
is a *jang* a vegetable,
a stringed musical instrument,
or an antique wooden chest?

What is the capital city
of the Philippines?

Ulaanbaatar is the capital
of which Asian country?

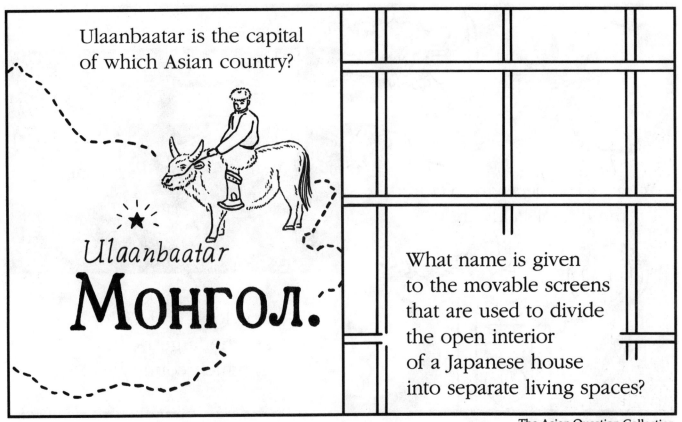

Ulaanbaatar

Монгол.

What name is given
to the movable screens
that are used to divide
the open interior
of a Japanese house
into separate living spaces?

101

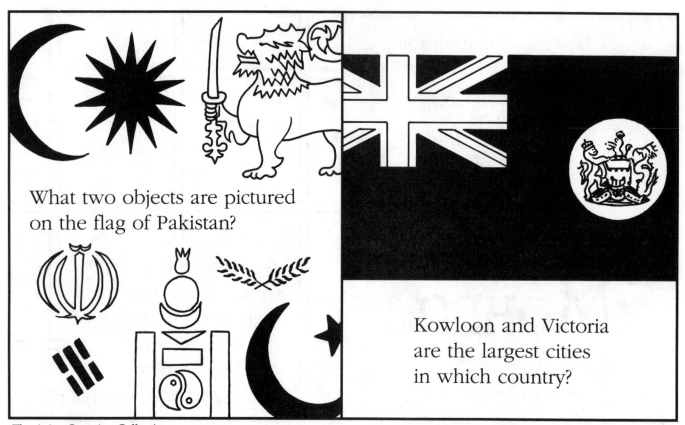

What two objects are pictured on the flag of Pakistan?

Kowloon and Victoria are the largest cities in which country?

1971

In 1971, East Pakistan became a separate nation. What is this nation called?

What is the capital of Thailand?

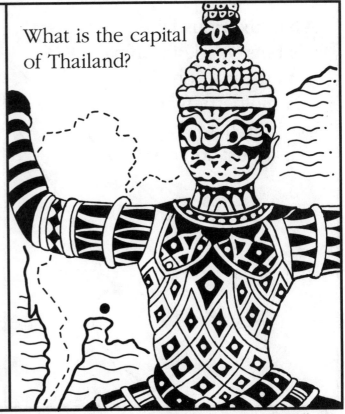

What luxurious fabric
has been made in China
from the cocoon
of a mulberry worm
for more than
four thousand years?

امرا ثومان وهزاره ولشكر ولمچينك كيرخان

What famous leader
united the scattered tribes
of the steppes and
turned them into Mongols?

The Japanese prize
a fancy cousin of the goldfish
for its colorful markings
and its longevity.
What is another name
for this Japanese carp?

What green gemstone
was often carved
by Chinese artisans
to create intricate
sculptures and
highly prized jewelry?

105

The Asian Question Collection
© 1994—The Learning Works, Inc.

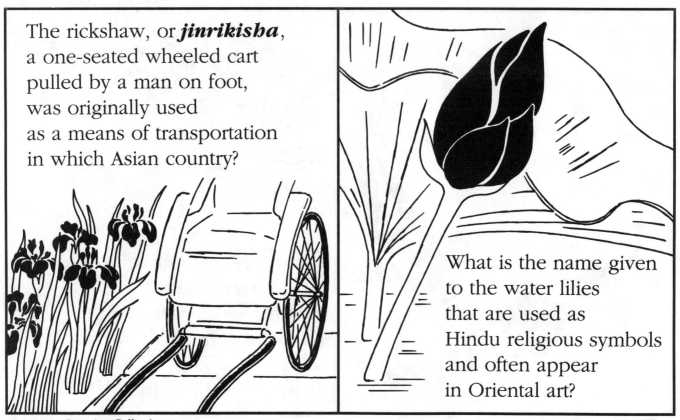

The rickshaw, or ***jinrikisha***, a one-seated wheeled cart pulled by a man on foot, was originally used as a means of transportation in which Asian country?

What is the name given to the water lilies that are used as Hindu religious symbols and often appear in Oriental art?

Which Asian people first used gunpowder in fireworks more than a thousand years ago?

Which Asian country is home to Ewha University, the largest women's university in the world?

대 학

The Asian Question Collection
© 1994—The Learning Works, Inc.

In 1894, China leased
the New Territories
to Hong Kong
for how many years?

What harvest festival,
celebrated by wearing
traditional dress and
visiting family tombs,
is often called the
Korean Thanksgiving Day?

Answer Key

Page 9
a. chopsticks
b. Japan

Page 10
a. Beijing
b. the Taj Mahal

Page 11
a. origami
b. reincarnation

Page 12
a. a teacher
b. Japan

Page 13
a. China
b. the head

Page 14
a. Vietnamese
b. giant pandas

Page 15
a. the crane
b. the Chinese New Year, or Spring Festival

Page 16
a. a drink
b. red and white

Page 17
a. bamboo shoots
b. tae kwon do

Page 18
a. the Pacific Ocean
b. a mosque

Page 19
a. a building
b. India

The Asian Question Collection
© 1994—The Learning Works, Inc.

Page 20
a. haiku
b. Hindi

Page 21
a. Mount Fuji, or Fujiyama
b. yoga

Page 22
a. the Chinese New Year
b. sukiyaki

Page 23
a. samurai
b. Indonesia

Page 24
a. China
b. monsoons

Page 25
a. sarongs
b. calligraphy

Page 26
a. the Arabian Sea
b. curry

Page 27
a. kimono
b. India

Page 28
a. sari
b. Mecca

Page 29
a. coconut
b. Mount Everest

Page 30
a. India
b. Urdu

Page 31
a. a wheel
b. the right

Page 32
a. Indonesia
b. chutney

Page 33
a. Indonesia
b. Brahman

Page 34
a. K^2, or Godwin Austen
b. by farming

Page 35
a. wear—they are sandals
b. yin and yang

Page 36
a. Pakistan
b. typhoon

Page 37
a. rice
b. tsunami

The Asian Question Collection
© 1994—The Learning Works, Inc.

Page 38
a. India
b. burka

Page 39
a. Mandarin Chinese
b. Vietnam

Page 40
a. the Koran
b. miso

Page 41
a. acupuncture
b. sashimi

Page 42
a. kami
b. Ramadan

Page 43
a. moon cakes
b. the Sikhs

Page 44
a. adabo
b. parliamentary

Page 45
a. Siddhartha Gautama
b. sepak tekraw

Page 46
a. monarchy
b. Confucius

Page 47
a. pencak silat
b. a huge plateau

Page 48
a. chima
b. sampans

Page 49
a. mah-jongg
b. Mohandas Gandhi

Page 50
a. Seoul
b. a wise teacher

Page 51
a. the dragon and the lion
b. tofu

Page 52
a. minarets
b. Hinduism

Page 53
a. Japan
b. satay

Page 54
a. tatami
b. 12 years and animals

Page 55
a. Pakistan
b. batik

The Asian Question Collection
© 1994—The Learning Works, Inc.

Page 56
a. obi
b. Shanghai

Page 57
a. a dynasty
b. the Philippines

Page 58
a. sumo wrestling
b. the Himalayas

Page 59
a. four main islands
b. October 1

Page 60
a. five days
b. the Grand Canal

Page 61
a. the Lantern Festival
b. Japan

Page 62
a. Great Britain
b. seven years

Page 63
a. the Doll Festival,
   or Hina Matsuri
b. the Forbidden City

Page 64
a. Pandit Jawaharlal Nehru
b. North Korea

Page 65
a. Syngman Rhee
b. good fortune and money

Page 66
a. ten major dynasties
b. Kabuki

Page 67
a. five tones
b. Undokai

Page 68
a. pansori
b. the rupee

Page 69
a. Mongolia
b. thirteen months

Page 70
a. Japan
b. Rama

Page 71
a. Minoru Yamasaki
b. jacks

Page 72
a. 1945
b. a red circle

Page 73
a. the sheng pipe
b. Islamabad

The Asian Question Collection
© 1994—The Learning Works, Inc.

Page 74
a. in China
b. river

Page 75
a. India and Pakistan
b. Hokkaido

Page 76
a. cloisonné
b. Jigoro Kano

Page 77
a. China
b. Sun Yat-sen

Page 78
a. Formosa
b. the yen

Page 79
a. the Shinano
b. Mao Zedong

Page 80
a. deserts
b. Burma

Page 81
a. Chinese dynasties
b. Chiang Kai-shek

Page 82
a. bonsai
b. sari

Page 83
a. Taiwan
b. the won, or hwan

Page 84
a. stupas
b. Shinto

Page 85
a. the Pekingese
b. Dacca

Page 86
a. Kublai Kahn
b. the land and peace

Page 87
a. the Yellow River
b. fusuma

Page 88
a. Mongolia
b. Maya Ying Lin

Page 89
a. South Korea
b. Zori

Page 90
a. wok
b. kimchi

Page 91
a. the Water Festival
b. India

The Asian Question Collection
© 1994—The Learning Works, Inc.

Page 92

a. the pyonjong, or bronze bells

b. communism

Page 93

a. the Hadam Festival, or the Three Games of Men

b. yellow

Page 94

a. the third, the fifth, and the seventh birthdays

b. Bangladesh

Page 95

a. futon

b. Thailand

Page 96

a. China

b. noodles

Page 97

a. China

b. kat

Page 98

a. Kampuchea

b. the Qing Ming Festival

Page 99

a. Ho Chi Minh City

b. the Festival of Lanterns

Page 100

a. an antique wooden chest

b. Manila

Page 101
a. Mongolia
b. shoji

Page 102
a. a crescent moon and a star
b. Hong Kong

Page 103
a. Bangladesh
b. Bangkok, or Krung Thep

Page 104
a. silk
b. Genghis Khan

Page 105
a. koi
b. jade

Page 106
a. Japan
b. lotus blossoms

Page 107
a. the Chinese
b. South Korea

Page 108
a. ninety-nine years
b. Chusok

The Asian Question Collection
© 1994—The Learning Works, Inc.

Nobue Maeno was born and educated in Tokyo, Japan, where she received a graphic design degree at Musashino College of Art. Since graduating from college, she has focused on illustrations, and her work has appeared in greeting cards, decorative rubber stamps, and numerous other products. Her love of nature and her diligent research of her subjects is reflected in her work. Nobue's combination of technique and imagination enhances her work as reflected in *The Asian Question Collection.*